JavaScript

Beginners Guide on Javascript
Programming

Nick Goddard

Table of Contents

Chapter 1

Introduction to JavaScript Programming Language

Welcome to the world of JavaScript, invented in 1995 by Brendan Eich it is still the most commonly used scripting language around today. It is high level, interpreted, cross platform and an open source programming language. In this tutorial series, we are going to learn JavaScript with practical examples. Before we dive in, let's go over some of the basics.

JavaScript is an OOP scripting language which mainly used in Web programming. It is responsible for making web pages interactive; in simple words "it tells web page what to perform". Like HTML defines the contents of the web page and CSS defines the layout, JavaScript make that web page work properly. JavaScript programs are the set of instructions which are executed in the order they are written so while coding, we should take care of the logical sequence. Do not get confused between Java and JavaScript, they both are technically different languages in respect of their design, however their standard libraries and syntaxes are same.

Now, let's learn how to install this amazing language on your computer and write our first JavaScript program.

Chapter 2

Development IDE setup

We are going to use eclipse as development IDE throughout this tutorials for explaining JavaScript program examples practically. The following are the steps to install eclipse and set up development environment for JavaScript.

Please follow the below steps:

1. Download the eclipse from below link. Choose the latest stable version of the eclipse and make sure that if your machine is 64-bit then choose 64-bit eclipse. In this tutorial, eclipse MARS.1 version is used.

https://eclipse.org/downloads

2. Click on the elipse.exe to open the eclipse which will ask to choose a local directory as its workspace as shown in the below screenshot.

3. Choose or create a directory on any available drive and click on the OK button to start eclipse.

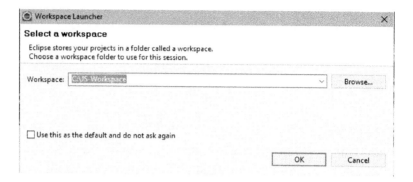

4. On the eclipse navigate as File -> New -> Static Web Project. Click on the link as shown below.

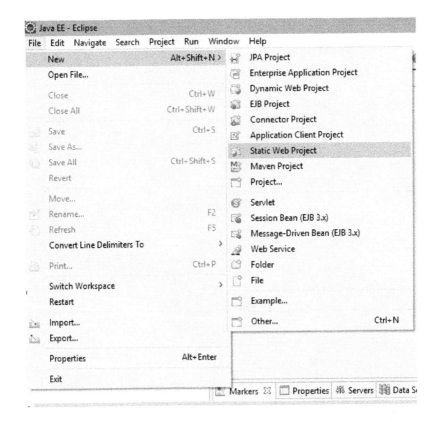

5. It will open up a dialogue box that will ask you to enter the name of the project. Please enter the project name and click on the 'Finish' button as shown below.

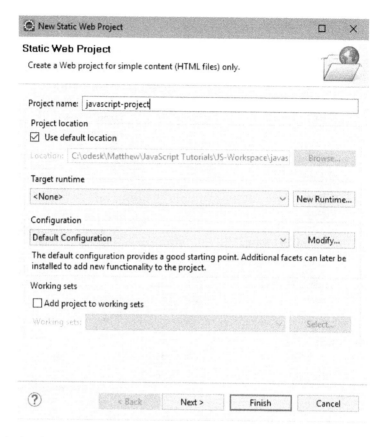

6. On the left hand side of Eclipse (project explorer), expand the project directory and right click on the 'WebContent' folder. To add a HTML file in the current project navigate as New -> HTML File as shown below.

7. It will open up a dialogue box that will ask you to enter the file name. Please enter the file name and click on the 'Finish' button as shown below. This will add up an HTML file to the current static web project.

At this point, you have successfully completed the development setup for JavaScript programming. In the next chapter, we are going to develop our first JavaScript program using this setup.

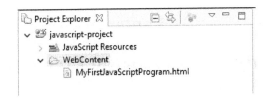

Chapter 3

My First JavaScript Program

JavaScript is a scripting language that could be injected anywhere on the web page between the <script>... </script> HTML tags, however it is always recommended to place in head section within <head> ... </head> tags.

While parsing the markup text (HTML) on the web page, when the browser program encounters the <script> tag, it start interpreting all the text present between these tags (till </script>) as a script. The script tag accepts the following two attributes.

> **Language** → this attribute specifies the type of scripting language that we are using. Its value is "*javascript*" for JavaScript language. In the latest versions of HTML, this attribute have been phased out.

> **Type** → this attribute indicates the type of scripting language that is in use and its value will be set to "*text/javascript*" for JavaScript language.

My First JavaScript Program

In the last chapter, we created an html file (MyFirstJavaScriptProgram.html). Let's use this file to write our first JavaScript program as shown below.

```
<!DOCTYPE html>
<html>
<head>
<meta charset="ISO-8859-1">
<title>My First JavaScript Program</title>
</head>
<body>
        <script language="javascript" type="text/javascript">
                document.write("Welcome to JavaScript First Program");
        </script>
</body>
</html>
```

Explanation of the JavaScript Code

Here, we have injected the JavaScript code between <body> ... </body> tags of the HTML. In the JavaScript code/script, we first declared the two attributes as discussed before and then with the help of the document object we are writing the message "Welcome to JavaScript First Program" on the web page.

Output

When we execute the above HTML program, the following will be the output.

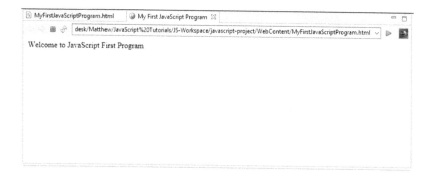

Whitespace and Line Breaks

We can use spaces, tabs, and newlines freely in our JavaScript program as these are ignored by browser parser program while parsing the JavaScript code. Also, we can freely format and indent our JavaScript programs in a tidy way that make the script very easy to maintain, read and understand.

Optional Semicolons

Usually, all JavaScript statements are ended with a semi-colon. But these semi-colons are optional when each of JavaScript statements are placed on a separate line. Using the semi-colons at the end of each JavaScript statement is considered as a good programming practice.

Case Sensitivity

JavaScript language is a case sensitive language. It means, the keywords, variables, function names, identifiers, etc. should be used with a consistent capitalization of letters. E.g. the identifier learn and LEARN are different from the point of view of the JavaScript language.

Comments in JavaScript

The following are the comment styles which are supported in the JavaScript language.

➤ Single line comment is declared as // (double slash).

➤ Multiple line comments is declared as /* JavaScript Statements on the multiple line */. It works for single line comment as well.

➤ It also recognized the HTML comment (opening sequence) <!--. JavaScript treats this as a single-line comment as it does with the // comment.

➤ The closing sequence --> of HTML is not recognized by JavaScript, Therefore, it should be written as //-->.

The following is an example that covers various JavaScript Comments.

```html
<!DOCTYPE html>
<html>
<head>
<meta charset="ISO-8859-1">
<title>JavaScript Comments</title>
</head>
<body>
        <script type="text/javascript">
        <!-- The opening sequence single line comment.
                The closing sequence HTML comment//-->


    // This is a single line comment.


    /*
    * This is a multiple line comment in JavaScript
    */
        </script>
</body>
</html>
```

Output

When we execute the above HTML program, the following will be the output (blank) since JavaScript interpreter has ignored all the comments.

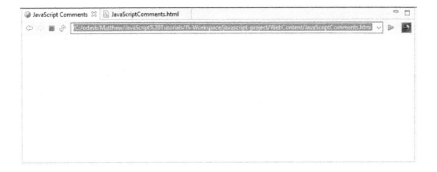

Chapter 4

JavaScript Syntax

Like any other programming language, JavaScript syntax has certain set of rules in which they are constructed.

Programs in JavaScript

A JavaScript program is a sequence of instructions which are parsed and executed by the browser program. These sequence of program instructions are known as statements.

> JavaScript is an objected oriented based programming language.

> JavaScript statements are usually separated by semicolons, however placing a semicolon at the end statement is optional.

```
<!DOCTYPE html>
<html>
<head>
<meta charset="ISO-8859-1">
<title>JavaScript Syntax</title>
        <script type="text/javascript">
                var a = 101;
                var b = 300;
```

```
            var sum = a + b;
      </script>
</head>
<body>
      <script type="text/javascript">
            document.write("sum of a + b = "+sum);
      </script>
</body>
</html>
```

Output

When we execute the above HTML program, the following will be the output.

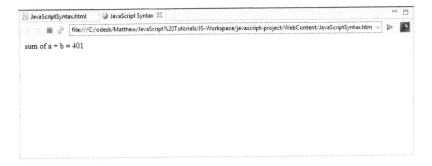

Statements in JavaScript

Statements in JavaScript programming language are composed of the following.

- ➢ Values

- ➢ Operators

- ➢ Expressions

- ➢ Keywords, and

- ➢ Comments.

Values in JavaScript

The following are the two types of values in JavaScript.

- ➢ Fixed values, and

- ➢ Variable values.

Literals are the fixed values and the variable values are known as variables.

Literals in JavaScript

The following are the rules for writing literals or fixed values in JavaScript.

- ➢ Numbers are defined with or without decimals.

- ➢ Strings are the text that are written within single or double quotes.

Variables in JavaScript

The following are the rules for writing variable values which are used to store data values in JavaScript.

- ➤ JavaScript language uses the *var* keyword to declare the variables.

- ➤ The value to a variable is assigned by an equal sign.

Operators in JavaScript

The following are the operators used in JavaScript language.

- ➤ **Assignment operator** (=) is used to assign values to a variable.

- ➤ **Arithmetic operators** (+-* /) are used for arithmetic operations such as addition, subtraction, multiplication, and division.

Expressions in JavaScript

Any expression in JavaScript language is a combination of values, variables, and operators. These together do computation. The computation is called an evaluation.

An expressions may also contain variable values such as numbers and strings. E.g., "Java" + "Script" will concatenate to "JavaScript".

Let's understand this with the help of the following example.

```
<!DOCTYPE html>
<html>
<head>
```

```
<meta charset="ISO-8859-1">
<title>JS Expressions</title>
    <script type="text/javascript">
            var a = 101; //variable, assignment operator and literal as
number.
            var b = 300;
            var addition = a + b;
            var str1 = "Java"; //variable, assignment operator and literal as
String.
            var str2 = "Script";
            var str3 = str1 + str2;
    </script>
</head>
<body>
    <script type="text/javascript">
            document.write("Addition of a + b = "+addition);
            document.write("<br>Concat of str1 + str2 = "+str3);
    </script>
</body>
</html>
```

Output

When we execute the above HTML program, the following will be the output. The output shows the addition and the concatenation operation.

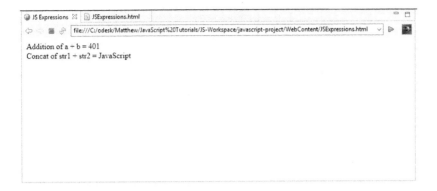

Keywords in JavaScript

Keywords in JavaScript language are used to identify the actions which are required to be performed. The *var* keyword directs the browser to create a new variable as JavaScript Identifiers. In JavaScript language, the identifiers are used to name variables (and keywords, and functions, and labels).

In JavaScript language, the first character must be a letter, an underscore (_), or a dollar sign ($) always. The subsequent characters may be letters, digits, underscores, or dollar signs.

Camel Case and JavaScript

There are the following three ways of joining multiple words into one variable name.

> **Hyphens** — E.g., first-address, second-address, visa-passport, city-name, etc.

➢ **Underscore** — E.g., first_address, second_address, visa_passport, city_name, etc.

➢ **Camel Case** — E.g., FirstAddress, SecondAddress, VisaPassport, InterName, etc. In JavaScript programming languages, the camel case often starts with a lowercase letter e.g., firstAddress, secondAddress, visaPassport, cityName, etc.

Character Set in JavaScript

JavaScript language uses the Unicode character set and it covers all the characters, punctuations, and symbols.

Chapter 5

JavaScript Enabling and Disabling

Web browsers such as Internet Explorer, Mozilla Firefox, Google Chrome, Opera, etc. come with built-in support for JavaScript. We can enable or disable the browser support for JavaScript manually. In this chapter we are going to discuss about the procedure of enabling and disabling JavaScript support in these browsers.

Enabling the JavaScript support in Internet Explorer

The following are the steps to turn on or enable JavaScript support in Internet Explorer.

> ➢ Navigate as Tools →Internet Options from the menu tab.

> ➢ From the dialog box, select the security tab.

> ➢ Click on the Custom Level button.

> ➢ Scroll down the menu and find the scripting option.

> ➢ Select to enable the radio button under the Active scripting caption.

> ➢ Lastly, click on the OK button to enable the JavaScript support on IE browser.

Disabling the JavaScript support in Internet Explorer

To turn off or disable the JavaScript support in Internet Explorer, follow the above steps and select to disable the radio button under Active scripting caption.

Enabling the JavaScript support in Mozilla Firefox

The following are the steps to turn on or enable the JavaScript support in Mozilla Firefox.

➤ Open a new tab and type *about: config* in the address bar.

➤ There we will find the following warning dialog Select and click on the button as *"I'll be careful, I promise!"* as shown below.

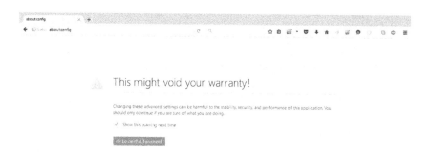

➤ Here, we will observe the list of configure options in the browser. In the search bar, type *javascript.enabled* as shown below.

> Here, we can find the option to *enable or disable* the javascript by right-clicking on the value of that option → select *toggle*.

> Upon clicking toggle, if the *javascript.enabled* is true then it will be converted to false. This will disable the JavaScript support to the Mozilla Firefox web browser.

Disabling the JavaScript support in Mozilla Firefox

The following are the steps to turn off or disable the JavaScript support in Mozilla Firefox. If javascript is disabled then it can be enabled upon *clicking toggle*, after following the similar steps as explained before.

Enabling or disabling the JavaScript support in Google Chrome

The following are the steps to enable or disable the JavaScript support in Google Chrome.

> Click on the Chrome menu present at the top right hand corner of the Chrome browser as shown below.

➤ Select the Settings and then click on *Show advanced settings* present at the end of the page.

➤ Under the Privacy section, click on the Content settings button as shown below.

> In the "Javascript" section on the Content settings, select "Do not allow any site to run JavaScript" or "Allow all sites to run JavaScript (recommended)" to disable and enable the JavaScript support on the Chrome browser respectively. The Content settings page is shown below.

Content settings   ×

Cookies

    ⦿ Allow local data to be set (recommended)

    ◯ Keep local data only until you quit your browser

    ◯ Block sites from setting any data

    ☐ Block third-party cookies and site data

    | Manage exceptions... | | All cookies and site data... |

Images

    ⦿ Show all images (recommended)

    ◯ Do not show any images

    | Manage exceptions... |

JavaScript

    ⦿ Allow all sites to run JavaScript (recommended)

    ◯ Do not allow any site to run JavaScript

    | Manage exceptions... |

Key generation

                                                 | Done |

Enabling or disabling the JavaScript support in Opera

The following are the steps to enable or disable the JavaScript support in Opera.

> ➢ Open the Opera browser and follow *Tools* → *Preferences* from the menu.

> ➢ Then, Select the *Advanced option* from the dialog box.

- Next, select the Content from the listed items.

- From there, select *Enable JavaScript* checkbox.

- Lastly, click OK button to enable the JavaScript support in Opera browser.

Similarly, to disable the JavaScript support in Opera browser, we should not select the *Enable JavaScript* checkbox and click on the OK button.

Warning for Non-JavaScript Browsers

When we have to do something very important by using the JavaScript, then we can show a warning message to the user by using the *<noscript>* tags. We can add a *noscript* block immediately after the script block as shown below.

```
<!DOCTYPE html>
<html>
<head>
<meta charset="ISO-8859-1">
<title>No Script tag</title>
</head>
<body>
    <script type="text/javascript">
    document.write("JavaScript Support is enabled on your browser!")
    </script>
    <noscript>
```

Please enable JavaScript support on your browser.

</noscript>

</body>

</html>

If any of the above browser does not support JavaScript or JavaScript support is disabled, then the message between the <noscript></noscript> tags will be shown on the screen.

Chapter 6

JavaScript Placement

Placement of JavaScript code in the HTML document is very flexible and can be placed in the following ways.

> **JavaScript in <head>...</head> section** — It is the most preferred way to include the JavaScript code in the head section of the HTML document. We can place the JavaScript code or functions in the head section and can access these functions on the web elements events as shown below.

```
<!DOCTYPE html>
<html>
<head>
<meta charset="ISO-8859-1">
<title>JS in head section</title>
	<script type="text/javascript">
		function showAlert(){
			alert ("This is an alert from Head section!");
		}
	</script>
```

```
</head>
<body>
        <input type="button" onclick="showAlert();" value="Call
JavaScript"/>
</body>
</html>
```

Output

When we execute the above HTML program, the following will be the
output. In the output, we can see the alert with a message as *"This is an alert
from Head section",* when we click on the button present on the web page.

> ➢ **JavaScript in <body>...</body> section** — we can also place the
>   JavaScript code in the body section of the HTML code, however this
>   approach is not preferred as we call JavaScript functions from body

section which are preferably defined in the head section of the HTML document.

```html
<!DOCTYPE html>
<html>
<head>
<meta charset="ISO-8859-1">
<title>JS Body</title>
</head>
<body>
        <script type="text/javascript">
                document.write("Welcome to JavaScript Tutorials!")
        </script>
        <p>Body section of the HTML document.</p>
</body>
</html>
```

Output

When we execute the above HTML program, the following will be the output. In the output, we can see the text *"Welcome to JavaScript Tutorials!"* written via JavaScript on the HTML page which is placed in its body section.

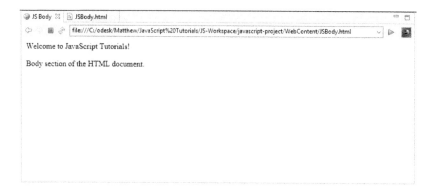

> ➤ **JavaScript in <body>...</body> and <head>...</head> sections —**
> in this approach, the JavaScript code is placed in both the head and the
> body section of the HTML document as shown in the following
> example.

```
<!DOCTYPE html>
<html>
<head>
<meta charset="ISO-8859-1">
<title>JS Head and Body</title>
        <script type="text/javascript">
                function showAlert(){
                        alert("This is an alert from Head section!");
                }
        </script>
</head>
<body>
        <script type="text/javascript">
                document.write("Welcome to JavaScript Tutorials!")
```

```
</script>
<p>Body section of the HTML document.</p>
<input type="button" onclick="showAlert();" value="Call
JavaScript"/>
</body>
</html>
```

Output

When we execute the above HTML program, the following will be the
output. In the output, we can see the text *"Welcome to JavaScript Tutorials!"*
written via JavaScript on the HTML page which is placed in its body
section. At the same time, when we click on the button, it will display an
alert message as *"This is an alert from Head section"*. This is the JavaScript
function called on click event of the button which is defined in the head
section of the HTML document.

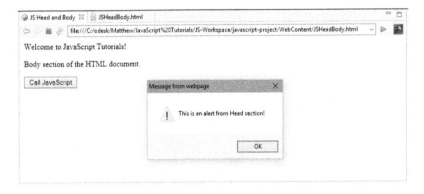

> **JavaScript placed in and external file and include in `<head>`...`</head>` section** — it is one of the best approach of placing all the JavaScript code in an external file which has file extension as **jscode.js** and we include this file in the head section of the HTML document. All the functions which are present in this file can be called on various web elements events defined in the body section of the HTML document. In the following example we have declared the function as *showAlert ()* in a separate file *"demo.js"* located in js directory.

function showAlert(){

        alert("This is an alert from Head section!");

   }

We are including this external JavaScript file in the head section of the HTML document as shown below.

```
<!DOCTYPE html>
<html>
<head>
<meta charset="ISO-8859-1">
<title>JS External File</title>
<script type="text/javascript" src="js/demo.js"></script>
</head>
<body>
        <input type="button" onclick="showAlert();" value="Call JavaScript"
/>
```

```
</body>
</html>
```

Output

When we execute the above HTML program, the following will be the output. In the output, we can see the alert with a message as *"This is an alert from Head section"*, this is the JavaScript function called on click event of the button which is defined in the external demo.js file and included in the head section head section of the HTML document. This works the same way as if we include the JavaScript function code in the head section of the HTML document.

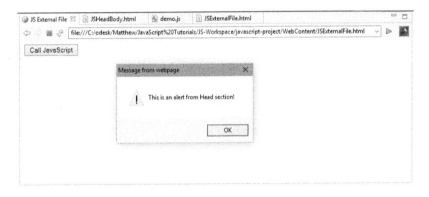

Chapter 7

JavaScript Variables

Datatypes in JavaScript

It is the characteristic of every programming language to support operations on the set of data types. These are the actual values which are defined and manipulated in any programming language. Like any other programming language, the JavaScript language allows us to work with the following three primitive data types.

> ➤ Numbers, e.g. 1, 23, 10.50, 23.8990 etc.

> ➤ Strings or text data, e.g. "JavaScript", "This is my language", etc.

> ➤ Boolean, as always it could be either true or false.

Apart from these three primitive datatypes, JavaScript language also defines the following two trivial data types. Each of which defines only a single value.

> ➤ Null.

> ➤ Undefined.

Also, JavaScript language supports a composite data type known as object. JavaScript objects will be covered in detail later in this tutorial.

This is to be noted that the JavaScript language does not make a distinction between integer values and floating-point values. JavaScript considers all numbers as the floating-point values. JavaScript represents numbers by using the 64-bit floating-point format which is defined by the IEEE 754 standard.

Variables in JavaScript

As discussed earlier, the JavaScript language has variables as data containers where we can place data into these containers and then refer this data by simply naming the container. We declare JavaScript variable with the var keyword as shown below.

```
<!DOCTYPE html>
<html>
<head>
<meta charset="ISO-8859-1">
<title>JavaScript Variables</title>
    <script type="text/javascript">
        var name = "Appy";
        var age = 21;
        var salary = 10000, expenses = 12000;
        alert ("Name: "+name+" Age: "+age+"\nSalary: "+ salary
            +" Expenses: "+expenses)
    </script>
</head>
<body>

</body>
```

`</html>`

Explanation of the JavaScript code

Storing of a value in a variable is known as variable initialization. We can do variable initialization at any point of time during the variable creation or the time when we need that variable.

For instance, we have created four variables in the above code and assigned value to each of these variables. E.g., *name* = *"Appy"*, *salary* = *10000, etc.*

Output

When we execute the above HTML program, the following will be the output. In the output, we are displaying the values that was assigned to the data container through an alert.

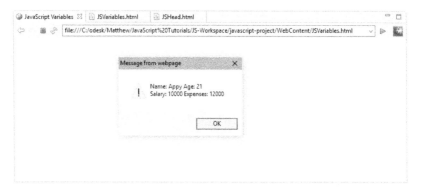

This is to be noted that the *var* keyword is used only for declaration or initialization, once for the life of any variable name in a HTML document.

We should not re-declare same variable more than once. In JavaScript, the variable can hold a value of any data type (number, string, etc.) as it is an untyped language. Unlike other typed languages (e.g., C, C++, JAVA, etc.), we don't need to tell JavaScript complier during variable declaration that what type of value the variable will hold. Also, the value type of a variable can change during the execution of a program which the JavaScript parser takes care of it automatically.

Variable Scope in JavaScript

The scope of a variable is defined as the region of the program in which it is defined. The JavaScript variables can have the following two scopes.

- ➢ **Global Variables scope** – is a global scope which means it can be defined anywhere in the JavaScript code and visible everywhere in the current HTML document.
- ➢ **Local Variables scope** – is a local variable which will be visible only within a function where it is defined. The function parameters are always local to the function.

This is to be noted that, within the body of a function, if both local and global variables are defined with the same name then local variable takes precedence over global variable always. Lets' understand this concept in the best way with the help of the following example.

```html
<!DOCTYPE html>
<html>
<head>
<meta charset="ISO-8859-1">
<title>Variable Scope</title>
</head>
    <script type = "text/javascript">
        var demoVar = "global scope"; // A global variable
        function checkVariableScope( ) {
          var demoVar = "local scope";  // A local variable
          document.write(demoVar);

        }
    </script>
<body onload = checkVariableScope();>


</body>
</html>
```

Output

When we execute the above HTML program, the following will be the output. In the output, we can observe the values as "local scope" as a local variable takes precedence over a global variable, if both are defined with the same name.

Variable Names in JavaScript

The rules should be obeyed while naming the variables in JavaScript language.

> No use of the variable name which are reserved keywords. These keywords are mentioned in the last section of this chapter. E.g. finally, goto, etc. variable names are invalid.

> Variable names in JavaScript language should never start with a number (0-9). However, they can begin with a letter or an underscore character. E.g. *10name* is an invalid variable but *_10name* is a valid variable name.

> Variable names in JavaScript are case-sensitive. E.g. *Address* and *address* are treated as two different variables names in JavaScript language.

Reserved Words in JavaScript

The following is a list of all the reserved words in JavaScript language. These reserved words cannot be used as JavaScript variables, loop labels, functions, or any object names.

abstract	debugger	final	instanceof	Public
boolean	default	finally	int	Return
break	delete	float	interface	Short
byte	do	for	long	Static
case	double	function	native	Super
catch	else	Goto	new	Switch
char	Enum	If	null	synchronized
class	Export	implements	package	This
const	extends	import	private	Throw
continue	FALSE	In	protected	Throws

Chapter 8

JavaScript Operators

When we add or subtract two values, e.g. adding 5 with 6 (i.e. 5 + 6), here '+' is known the operator and (5 + 6) is known as expression. The JavaScript language supports the following types of operators.

Arithmetic Operators

The following are the arithmetic operators which are supported by the JavaScript language.

S No.	Arithmetic Operator	Description	Example
1.	+ (Addition)	It is used to add two operands.	X + Y
2.	- (Subtraction)	It is used to subtract the second operand from first operand.	X - Y
3.	* (Multiplication)	It is used to multiply two operands.	X * Y
4.	/ (Division)	It is used to divide two operands i.e. divide numerator with the denominator.	X / Y

5.	% (Modulus)	This operator outputs the remainder of an integer division.	X % Y
6.	++ (Increment)	It increase the integer value by 1.	X++
7.	-- (Decrement)	It decrease the integer value by 1.	Y--

Comparison Operators

The following are the comparison operators which are supported by the JavaScript language.

S No.	Comparison Operator	Description	Example
1	= = (Equal)	This operator is used to Check if the value of two operands are equal or not, if both values are equal, then the condition becomes true.	Ex: (X == Y) is not true.
2	!= (Not Equal)	This operator is used to check if the value of two operands are equal or not, if the values	Ex: (X! = Y) is true.

		are unequal, then the condition becomes true.	
3	> (Greater than)	This operator is used to check if the value of the left operand is greater than the value of the right operand, if it is the case, then the condition becomes true.	Ex: (X > Y) is not true.
4	< (Less than)	This operator is used to check if the value of the left operand is less than the value of the right operand, if it is the case, then the condition becomes true.	Ex: (X < Y) is true.
5	>= (Greater than or Equal to)	This operator is used to check if the value of the left operand is greater than or equal to the value of the right operand, if it is the case, then the condition becomes true.	Ex: (X >= Y) is not true.
6	<= (Less than or Equal to)	This operator is used to check if the value of the left operand is less than or equal to the value of the right operand, if it is the	Ex: (X <= Y) is true.

case,   then   the   condition
becomes true.

Logical (or Relational) Operators

The following are the logical or relational operators which are supported by the JavaScript language.

S No.	Logical Operator	Description	Example
1	&& (Logical AND)	If both the operands are non-zero, then this operator makes the condition becomes true.	Ex: (X && Y) is true.
2	|| (Logical OR)	If any of the two operands are non-zero, then this operator makes the condition becomes true.	Ex: (X || Y) is true.
3	! (Logical NOT)	This operator reverses the logical state of its operand. If a condition is true, then the Logical NOT operator will make it false and vice-versa.	Ex :!(X && Y) is false.

Assignment Operators

The following are the assignment operators which are supported by the JavaScript language.

S No.	Assignment Operator	Description	Example
1.	=(Simple Assignment)	This operator is used to assign the value from the right side operand to the left side operand.	Ex: Z = X - Y will assign the value of X - Y into Z variable.
2.	+= (Add and Assignment)	This operator is used to add the right operand to the left operand and assigns the result to the left operand.	Ex: Z += X is equivalent to Z = Z + X
3.	−= (Subtract and Assignment)	This operator is used to subtract the right operand from the left operand and assigns the result to the left operand.	Ex: Z -= X is equivalent to Z = Z − X
4.	*= (Multiply and Assignment)	This operator is used to multiply the right operand with the left operand and assigns	Ex: Z *= X is equivalent to Z = Z * X

		the result to the left operand.	
5.	/= (Divide and Assignment)	This operator is used to divide the left operand with the right operand and assigns the result to the left operand.	Ex: Z /= X is equivalent to Z = Z / X
6.	%= (Modules and Assignment)	This operator is used to takes the modulus using two operands and assigns the result to the left operand.	Ex: Z %= X is equivalent to Z= Z % X

Conditional (or ternary) Operators

The following is the conditional or ternary operator which is supported by the JavaScript language.

S No.	Conditional Operator	Description	Example
1.	? : (Conditional)	If Condition is true? Then value X : Otherwise value Y.	Ex: (X > Y)? "yes" : "No"

Bitwise Operators

The following are the bitwise operators which are supported by the JavaScript language.

S No.	Bitwise Operator	Description	Example
1.	& (Bitwise AND)	This operator is used to perform a Boolean AND operation on each bit of its integer arguments.	Ex: (X & Y) is 2.
2.	| (Bitwise OR)	This operator is used to perform a Boolean OR operation on each bit of its integer arguments.	Ex: (X | Y) is 3.
3.	^ (Bitwise XOR)	This operator is used to perform a Boolean exclusive OR operation on each bit of its integer arguments. Exclusive OR means that either operand one is true or operand two is true, but not both.	Ex: (X ^ Y) is 1.
4.	~ (Bitwise Not)	Bitwise Not is a unary operator	X / Y

	Ex: (~B) is -4.	and operates by reversing all the bits in the operand.	
5.	<< (Left Shift)	This operator is used move all the bits in its first operand to the left by the number of places specified in the second operand. New bits are filled with zeros. Shifting a value left by one position is equivalent to multiplying it by 2, shifting two positions is equivalent to multiplying by 4, and so on.	Ex: (X << 1) is 4.
6.	>> (Right Shift)	In Binary Right Shift Operator, the left operand's value is moved right by the number of bits specified by the right operand.	Ex: (X >> 1) is 1.
7.	>>> (Right shift with Zero)	This operator is just like the >> operator, except that the bits shifted in on the left are always zero.	Ex: (X >>> 1) is 1.

Chapter 9

JavaScript Decision Making

While writing a program, most of the time we face a situation where we have to make a decision. Decision making is the anticipation of conditions that could occur while execution of a program and there is a need to specify some actions according to those conditions.

In a decision making structures, there is a condition which is either a single expression or multiple expressions. This condition when evaluated produce either TRUE or FALSE as outcome. Based on the outcome, we need to determine which action to take and which statements to execute. Refer the figure below to understand it clearly.

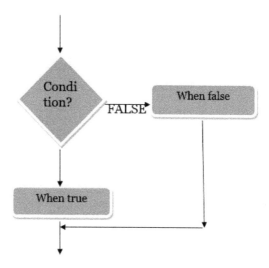

Like any other programming language, the JavaScript language supports conditional statements which are used to perform different actions based on different conditions. The following are the conditional statement supported by the JavaScript language.

> if statement.

> if...else statement

> if...else if... statement.

> Switch case statement

Let's understand these statements with the help of a JavaScript program.

- ➤ **if statement** — the *if* statement is a basic control statement which allows the JavaScript code to make decisions and execute statements based on required condition. The following is the syntax.

Syntax and Example

```html
<!DOCTYPE html>
<html>
<head>
<meta charset="ISO-8859-1">
<title>Basic IF Statement</title>
</head>
<body>
        <script type="text/javascript">
        var salary = 10000;
        var expenses = 12000;
        if( expenses > salary ){
           document.write("<b>Please either start earning more or spend
less!</b>");
           }
    </script>
        <p>We are inside the body section...</p>
</body>
</html>
```

Output

When we execute the above HTML program, the following will be the output. Since the condition in the "*if*" statement is true therefore, it will write the given text on the HTML page.

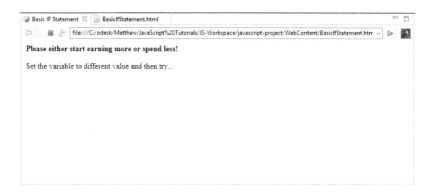

> ➤ **if...else statement** – the 'if...else' statement is the another form of the control statement which allows the JavaScript code to execute statements in a more controlled way. The following is syntax and example.

Syntax and example

```
<!DOCTYPE html>
<html>
<head>
```

```html
<meta charset="ISO-8859-1">
<title>If Else Statement</title>
</head>
<body>
    <script type="text/javascript">
    var salary = 12000;
    var expenses = 10000;
    if( expenses > salary ){
        document.write("<b>Please either start earning more or spend less!</b>");
    }
    else {
        document.write("<b>You have enough money to spend!</b>");
    }
    </script>
    <p>We are inside the body section...</p>
</body>
</html>
```

Output

When we execute the above HTML program, the following will be the output. Since the condition in the "*if*" statement is false therefore, it has entered the else block and has written the given text on the HTML page.

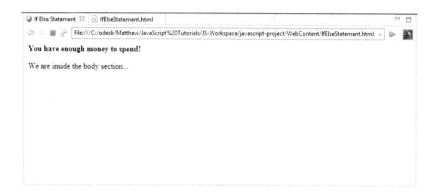

You have enough money to spend!

We are inside the body section...

> **if...else if... statement** —the *if...else if...* statement is another advanced form of *if...else* which allows the JavaScript code to make a correct decision out of the defined several conditions. It has the series of if statements in which each if is a part of the else clause of the last statement. These Statement(s) are executed based on the true condition, if it happens that none of the conditions is true, then the code present in the else block will be executed. The following is the syntax and example.

Syntax and Example

```
<!DOCTYPE html>
<html>
<head>
<meta charset="ISO-8859-1">
<title>If Else If Statement</title>
```

```
</head>
<body>
    <script type="text/javascript">
    var salary = 12000;
    var expenses = 10000;
    if( expenses > salary ){
        document.write("<b>Please either start earning more or spend
less!</b>");
    }
    else if (salary > 13000){
        document.write("<b>You have enough money to spend!</b>");
    }
    else {
        document.write("<b>Although you have enough money but you
need to be careful!</b>");
    }
    </script>
    <p>We are inside the body section...</p>
</body>
</html>
```

Output

When we execute the above HTML program, the following will be the output. Since the condition in the "*if*" statement is false therefore, it has entered the else if block where there is another condition that happens to be false. Hence, it has written the given text on the HTML page which is present in the last else block.

Switch Case Statement

Starting with the JavaScript 1.2 version, it has started supporting a switch statement that handles exactly the situation as implemented by the repeated if...else if statements.

A switch statement is used to give an expression that evaluate the several different statements based on the value of the expression. The JavaScript interpreter inspects each case against the return value of the expression until a match is found. If no match is found then it uses the default condition.

Also, there is a *break* statements which is present at the end of a case code statement. If break is not declared here, then the interpreter would continue executing all the statement in each of the following cases.

The following is the syntax and example of switch case statement.

```html
<!DOCTYPE html>
<html>
<head>
<meta charset="ISO-8859-1">
<title>Switch Case Statement</title>
</head>
<body>
        <script type="text/javascript">
            var expensecode='X';
        document.write("Entering the switch block<br />");
        switch (expensecode)
        {
        case 'X': document.write("<b>Please either start earning more or spend less!</b>");
            break;

        case 'Y': document.write("<b>You have enough money to spend!</b>");
            break;

        case 'Z': document.write("<b>Although you have enough money but you need to be careful!</b>");
            break;

        default:  document.write("No match found!<br />")
```

```
        }
        document.write("<br>Exiting the switch block<br />");
    </script>
        <p>We are inside the body section...</p>
</body>
</html>
```

Output

When we execute the above HTML program, the following will be the
output. The program has written the text on HTML page whose case
character ('X') is matching.

Chapter 10

JavaScript Loops

When any program is executed, it runs sequentially. The statement which appears first in the sequence is executed first then the next statement and so on till the last statement of the program. Many times there is a requirement to run same block of code in a program multiple times then there arises a need of a control structure known as loops.

A loop makes a statement or group of statements in a block of code to execute multiple times if the condition is true and exits the loop when the condition becomes false. Such loop is illustrated in the below diagram.

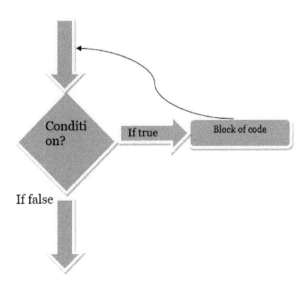

Like any other programming language, the JavaScript support looping and the following types of loops and the loop control statements.

- ➢ While loop

- ➢ Do…while loop

- ➢ For loop

- ➢ for...in loop

- ➢ Loop control statements

While loop statement

While loop is the most basic loop in JavaScript language. This loop execute a statement or piece of code block repeatedly as long as an expression is held true. The loop terminates, once the expression is false. The following is the syntax and the example of while loop statement.

```html
<!DOCTYPE html>
<html>
<head>
<meta charset="ISO-8859-1">
<title>While Loop</title>
</head>
<body>
    <script type="text/javascript">
    var counter = 0;
    document.write("Entering while Loop!");
```

```
        while (counter < 5){
        document.write("Current Counter is : " + counter + "<br />");
        counter++;
        }
        document.write("Exiting while Loop!");
    </script>
        <p>We are inside body section...</p>
</body>
</html>
```

Output

When we execute the above HTML program, the following will be the output. The counter will write 5 times on the HTML page as it held its condition true 5 times.

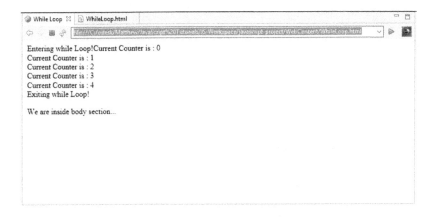

Do...while loop statement

The do...while loop is similar to that of the while loop except that the condition check in case of do...while loop happens at the end of the loop. This means that the code block inside the loop will always be executed at least once, even if the condition is false. The following is the syntax and the example of while loop statement.

```html
<!DOCTYPE html>
<html>
<head>
<meta charset="ISO-8859-1">
<title>Do While Loop</title>
</head>
<body>
    <script type="text/javascript">
    var counter = 0;
    document.write("Entering while Loop!");
    do {
      document.write("Current Counter is : " + counter + "<br />");
      counter++;
    }
    while (counter < 5)
    document.write("Exiting while Loop!");
  </script>
    <p>We are inside body section...</p>
</body>
</html>
```

Output

When we execute the above HTML program, the following will be the output. The counter will write 5 times on the HTML page as it held its condition true 5 times including the first no check condition.

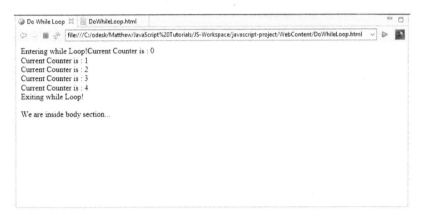

For loop statement

The 'for' loop is very important and mostly used looping statement in JavaScript programming. The command has the following three important parts.

> **Loop initialization** — it is where we initialize our counter value to a starting initial value. This statement is executed before the looping begins.

- ➤ **Test statement** — it has the actual condition which is evaluated to be true or false. If this condition evaluates to be true, then the block of code inside the loop will be executed, otherwise, if false then the control will exit the loop.

- ➤ **Iteration statement** — it is place where we increase or decrease the counter value which was initialized in the first statement.

The good part of for loop is that we can put all of these three statement parts in a single line which is separated by semicolons. The following is the syntax and the example.

```html
<!DOCTYPE html>
<html>
<head>
<meta charset="ISO-8859-1">
<title>For Loop</title>
</head>
<body>
    <script type="text/javascript">
    document.write("Entering while Loop!");
    for(counter = 0;counter < 5; counter++){
      document.write("Current Counter is : " + counter + "<br />");
    }
    document.write("Exiting while Loop!");
  </script>
    <p>We are inside body section...</p>
</body>
```

```
</html>
```

Output

When we execute the above HTML program, the following will be the output. The counter will write 5 times on the HTML page as it held its condition true 5 times till the counter value becomes 5 and the loop exits.

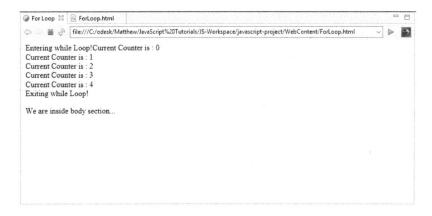

For...in loop statement

The *for...in* loop is used only in the special cases where there is need to loop through an object's properties. The following is the syntax and the example for *for...in* loop.

```
<!DOCTYPE html>
<html>
<head>
<meta charset="ISO-8859-1">
```

```
<title>For In Statement</title>
</head>
<body>
    <script type="text/javascript">
        var prop;
        document.write("Object Properties of Navigator <br /> ");
        document.write ("Entering the loop!");
        for (prop in navigator) {
           document.write(prop);
           document.write("<br />");
        }
        document.write ("Exiting the loop!");
    </script>
    <p>We are in the body section...</p>
</body>
</html>
```

Output

When we execute the above HTML program, the following will be the output. In the output, we have iterated through the "navigator" object and displayed all the object properties of the web browser's navigator object.

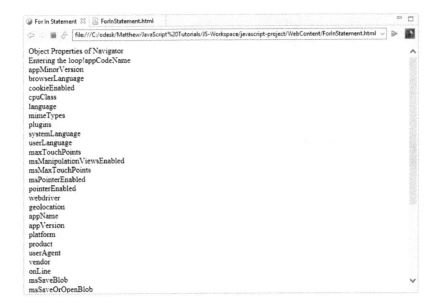

Summary of Loops in JavaScript

Loop Type	Description
while loop	While loop type, repeats a statement or group of statements while a given condition is true. It tests the condition each time it executes the loop body and it exits the loop when condition becomes false.
for loop	For loop type executes a sequence of statements multiple times and abbreviates the code that manages the loop variable.
nested loops	It is a loop within a loop. In JavaScript, we can use a while loop in another while or for loop or for loop in

	another while or for loop.

Loop control statements

Loop control statements in JavaScript language are used to change execution from its normal sequence. When such execution leaves a scope, all automatic objects that were created in that scope are destroyed or removed.

In JavaScript language, the following loop control statements are supported.

Control Statement	Description
break statement	The break statement in JavaScript is used to terminate the loop statement and transfers execution to the statement immediately following after the end of loop.
continue statement	The continue statement in JavaScript is used to cause the loop to skip the remainder of its body and immediately retest its condition prior to reiterating the looping body.

Let's understand these loop control statement in a better way with the help of the following example.

```
<!DOCTYPE html>
<html>
<head>
<meta charset="ISO-8859-1">
<title>Loop Control Statement</title>
```

```
</head>
<body>
        <script type="text/javascript">
        var counter = 0;
        document.write("Entering while Loop!<br>");
        while (counter < 5){
            if (counter == 3){
                    counter++;
                    continue;
            }
            if (counter == 4){
                break;
          }
        document.write("Current Counter is : " + counter + "<br />");
        counter++;
        }
        document.write("Exiting while Loop!");
    </script>
        <p>We are inside body section...</p>
</body>
</html>
```

Output

When we execute the above HTML program, the following will be the output. In the output, we can see that the counter value are printed 3 times (0, 1 and 2) and then the loop exited. This is because when the counter value has become 3, we are executing continue loop control statement where it has incremented the counter to 4 and has skipped the document writing part and recheck the condition. When the counter value has become 4, we are executing the break loop control statement which will eventually exit out from the current loop skipping document writing statement again.

Chapter 11

JavaScript Functions

A function may be defined as a block of code that is well organized and reusable multiple times to perform a number of operations in a program that demands high modularity and reusability. It eliminates the need of writing the same piece of code again and again and helps the programmers in writing modular codes. With the concept of functions, it is possible for a programmer to break a big program into a number of small and manageable functions which eventually reduces the redundancy.

Like any other programming language, the JavaScript language also supports the required features to write modular code by using functions. Since the beginning of this tutorials, we are using functions like "alert ()" and "write ()" which gives us a little hint about the operations of the functions. These functions are in-built JavaScript functions. In JavaScript language, we can write our own functions like any other programming language that we are going to learn in this chapter.

Function Definition

Functions are useable at any point in the code for which we have to define them only once. In JavaScript, we define a function by using the function keyword which is followed by a unique function name, a list of parameters (that could be empty), and a statement block surrounded by curly braces. The following is the syntax and the example of the JavaScript function.

```
<!DOCTYPE html>
<html>
<head>
<meta charset="ISO-8859-1">
<title>Function Definition</title>
<script type="text/javascript">
        function sayHelloToJavaScript() {
                alert ("Welcome to the world of JavaScript!");
        }
</script>
</head>
<body>

</body>
</html>
```

Calling a Function

We can invoke a JavaScript function later in the script or on the HTML web elements events, we simply need to write the name of that function as shown in the following code.

```
<!DOCTYPE html>
<html>
<head>
```

```
<meta charset="ISO-8859-1">
<title>Function Definition</title>
<script type="text/javascript">
        function sayHelloToJavaScript() {
                alert ("Welcome to the world of JavaScript!");
        }
</script>
</head>
<body>

</body>
</html>
```

Output

When we execute the above HTML program, the following will be the output. Here, we are calling the JavaScript function on click event on the button which display an alert with message which is picked up from the head section of the HTML where JavaScript function is defined.

Function Parameters

Till this point, we have used the functions which were without the input parameters. In a JavaScript function, we can pass different parameters while calling it. The values of the passed parameters can be used inside the function and we can do the manipulation on these parameters. A function can take none to multiple parameters. Multiple parameters in a function are separated by commas. The following is the syntax and the example of the parameterized function.

```
<!DOCTYPE html>
<html>
<head>
<meta charset="ISO-8859-1">
<title>Parameterized Function</title>
<script type="text/javascript">
        function sayHelloToJavaScript(message,entity,lang) {
                alert(message+" to the "+entity+" world of "+lang+"!");
        }
</script>
</head>
<body>
        <input type="button"
onclick="sayHelloToJavaScript('Welcome','World','JavaScript');"
value="Call JavaScript"/>
        <p>Body section of the HTML document.</p>
```

```
</body>
</html>
```

Output

When we execute the above HTML program, the following will be the output. Here, we are calling the parameterized JavaScript function on click event on the button which display an alert with message which is picked up from the head section of the HTML where JavaScript function is defined. Here, we are passing three parameters in the function which we are displaying in the alert message.

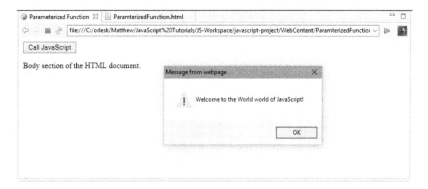

The return Statement

A JavaScript function can return a value and this return statement is optional. Return statement is used when we want to return a value from a function. It should always be the last statement in a JavaScript function. Let's understand the use of return function with the help of the following example.

```html
<!DOCTYPE html>
<html>
<head>
<meta charset="ISO-8859-1">
<title>Return Function</title>
<script type="text/javascript">

        function concatString(message,entity,lang) {
                var str = message+entity+lang;
                return str;
        }
        function writeToDoc(message,entity,lang){
                concatStr= concatString(message,entity,lang);
                document.write (concatStr);
        }
</script>
</head>
<body>
        <input type="button" onclick="writeToDoc('Welcome to the ','World
of','JavaScript!');" value="Call JavaScript"/>
        <p>Body section of the HTML document.</p>
</body>
</html>
```

Output

When we execute the above HTML program, the following will be the output. Here, we are calling the JavaScript function on click event on the button which display the message on the HTML page which is picked up from the head section of the HTML where JavaScript function is defined. Here, we have passed three strings in the *"writeToDoc"* function as the parameters which calls "concatString*"* function which returns the concatenated string that is written on the document.

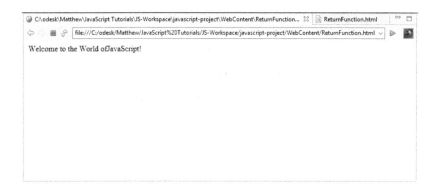

Chapter 12

JavaScript Events

JavaScript Events are the means through which JavaScript interacts with the HTML document. These events are triggered when any value is manipulated on the HTML page either by the user or the browser. E.g. when we load a HTML page, it is known as an event. Similarly, when we click a button on the page, it is also an event. We can think of other examples of events such as pressing any key, submitting a form through button, changing the size of a window, etc.

Programmers can use these JavaScript events to trigger and execute JavaScript coded responses. These responses includes closing of a window on button click, displaying alert message to user, validating the form data, etc.

JavaScript events are the part of the Document Object Model (DOM) Level 3. All HTML web element contains a set of events which are capable of triggering JavaScript function code.

The following are the few examples to understand the relation between Event and invoking JavaScript function code.

> ➤ **onclick Event Type**

It is the most frequently used event type that triggers a JavaScript code when we left click the button of mouse on HTML page or web element. Here, we can put our validation, etc., against this event type. The following example demonstrates this event.

```html
<!DOCTYPE html>
<html>
<head>
<meta charset="ISO-8859-1">
<title>On Click Events</title>
<script type="text/javascript">
        function showAlert() {
                alert("This is an alert on onclick event!");
        }
</script>
</head>
<body>
        <input type="button" onclick="showAlert();" value="Call JavaScript"
/>
</body>
</html>
```

Output

When we execute the above HTML program, the following will be the output. We are invoking a JavaScript function "showAlert" through a button onclick event which is displaying a message on an alert dialogue box.

> ### ➢ onsubmit Event Type

It is an event type that comes into play while we submit a HTML form. We can also put our form validation against this event type.

In the following example, we are demonstrating how onsubmit event is triggered. We can call a "validate ()" function before submitting a form data to the webserver. The form will be submitted only if the "validate ()" function returns true, otherwise it will not be submitted at all.

```
<!DOCTYPE html>
<html>
<head>
<meta charset="ISO-8859-1">
<title>On Submit Events</title>
    <script type="text/javascript">
        function validation() {
```

```
if(document.form1.textbox1.value != ''){
        alert('Validation Passed');
        return true;
    }
    else{
        alert ('Text Box field cannot be empty!');
        return false;
    }
}
</script>
</head>
<body>
    <form name="form1" method="GET" action="onClickEvent.html"
onsubmit="return validation()">
    <input type="text" name="textbox1"/>
    <input type="submit" value="Submit" />
    </form>
</body>
</html>
```

Output

When we execute the above HTML program, the following will be the output. Here, we are validating that the text box element cannot be blank or empty, if no value is entered in it and the submit button is clicked then it will return false to the form submission and display an alert message as "Text Box field cannot be empty!"

> ➤ **onmouseover and onmouseout Event Types**

These two are popular mouse event types which help us to create nice effects with images or texts. The onmouseover event gets triggered when we bring our mouse over any web element on the HTML page and the onmouseout event gets triggered when we move our mouse out from that web element. The following example demonstrates these events.

```
<!DOCTYPE html>
<html>
<head>
<meta charset="ISO-8859-1">
<title>Mouse Over and Out</title>
    <script type="text/javascript">
        function hoverMouse() {
            alert ("Doing the Mouse Over");
        }

        function hoverMouseOut() {
```

```
        alert ("Taking the Mouse Out");
      }
    </script>
  </head>
  <body>
    <div onmouseover="hoverMouse();" onmouseout="hoverMouseOut();">
      <h1> Bring your Mouse here to see the change </h1>
    </div>
  </body>
</html>
```

Output

When we execute the above HTML program, the following will be the output. Here, when we bring the mouse over on the heading division, we can see the alert messaging getting invoked. Similarly, when we mouse out the region, we see another alert for moving the mouse out of heading division.

Standard Events present in HTML 5

The following ae the standard HTML 5 events attribute. All of these attributes have value as script which indicates a Javascript function which is to be invoked and executed against the triggered event.

Event Attribute	Value	Description
Offline	script	This attribute triggers when the document goes offline.
Onabort	script	This attribute triggers on an abort event.
Onafterprint	script	This attribute triggers after the document is printed.
onbeforeonload	script	This attribute triggers before the document loads.
Onbeforeprint	script	This attribute triggers before the document is printed.
Onblur	script	This attribute triggers when the window loses focus.
Oncanplay	script	This attribute triggers when media can start

		play, but might has to stop for buffering.
oncanplaythrough	script	This attribute triggers when media can be played to the end, without stopping for buffering.
Onchange	script	This attribute triggers when an element changes.
Onclick	script	This attribute triggers on a mouse click.
oncontextmenu	script	This attribute triggers when a context menu is triggered.
Ondblclick	script	This attribute triggers on a mouse double-click.
Ondrag	script	This attribute triggers when an element is dragged.
Ondragend	script	This attribute triggers at the end of a drag operation.
Ondragenter	script	This attribute triggers when an element has

been dragged to a valid drop target.

Ondragleave	script	This attribute triggers when an element is being dragged over a valid drop target.
Ondragover	script	This attribute triggers at the start of a drag operation.
Ondragstart	script	This attribute triggers at the start of a drag operation.
Ondrop	script	This attribute triggers when dragged element is being dropped.
Ondurationchange	script	This attribute triggers when the length of the media is changed.
Onemptied	script	This attribute triggers when a media resource element suddenly becomes empty.
Onended	script	This attribute triggers when media has reach the end.
Onerror	script	This attribute triggers when an error occur.

Onfocus	script	This attribute triggers when the window gets focus.
onformchange	script	This attribute triggers when a form changes.
Onforminput	script	This attribute triggers when a form gets user input.
Onhaschange	script	This attribute triggers when the document has change.
Oninput	script	This attribute triggers when an element gets user input.
Oninvalid	script	This attribute triggers when an element is invalid.
Onkeydown	script	This attribute triggers when a key is pressed.
Onkeypress	script	This attribute triggers when a key is pressed and released.
Onkeyup	script	This attribute triggers when a key is released.

onload	script	This attribute triggers when the document loads.
Onloadeddata	script	This attribute triggers when media data is loaded.
onloadedmetadata	script	This attribute triggers when the duration and other media data of a media element is loaded.
Onloadstart	script	This attribute triggers when the browser starts to load the media data.
Onmessage	script	This attribute triggers when the message is triggered.
onmousedown	script	This attribute triggers when a mouse button is pressed.
onmousemove	script	This attribute triggers when the mouse pointer moves.
Onmouseout	script	This attribute triggers when the mouse pointer moves out of an element.

Onmouseover	script	This attribute triggers when the mouse pointer moves over an element.
Onmouseup	script	This attribute triggers when a mouse button is released.
onmousewheel	script	This attribute triggers when the mouse wheel is being rotated.
Onoffline	script	This attribute triggers when the document goes offline.
Onoine	script	This attribute triggers when the document comes online.
Ononline	script	This attribute triggers when the document comes online.
Onpagehide	script	This attribute triggers when the window is hidden.
Onpageshow	script	This attribute triggers when the window becomes visible.

Onpause	script	This attribute triggers when media data is paused.
Onplay	script	This attribute triggers when media data is going to start playing.
Onplaying	script	This attribute triggers when media data has start playing.
Onpopstate	script	This attribute triggers when the window's history changes.
onprogress	script	This attribute triggers when the browser is fetching the media data.
Onratechange	script	This attribute triggers when the media data's playing rate has changed.
onreadystatechange	script	This attribute triggers when the ready-state changes.
Onredo	script	This attribute triggers when the document performs a redo.

Onresize	script	This attribute triggers when the window is resized.
Onscroll	script	This attribute triggers when an element's scrollbar is being scrolled.
Onseeked	script	This attribute triggers when a media element's seeking attribute is no longer true, and the seeking has ended.
Onseeking	script	This attribute triggers when a media element's seeking attribute is true, and the seeking has begun.
Onselect	script	This attribute triggers when an element is selected.
Onstalled	script	This attribute triggers when there is an error in fetching media data.
Onstorage	script	This attribute triggers when a document loads.
Onsubmit	script	This attribute triggers when a form is submitted.

Onsuspend	script	This attribute triggers when the browser has been fetching media data, but stopped before the entire media file was fetched.
Ontimeupdate	script	This attribute triggers when media changes its playing position.
Onundo	script	This attribute triggers when a document performs an undo.
Onunload	script	This attribute triggers when the user leaves the document.
onvolumechange	script	This attribute triggers when media changes the volume, also when volume is set to "mute".
Onwaiting	script	This attribute triggers when media has stopped playing, but is expected to resume.

Chapter 13

JavaScript Dialogue Boxes

Dialogue boxes are used in JavaScript to raise a warning using alert, or ask for a confirmation, or to accept an input from the user. To support these features, JavaScript has three types of dialogue boxes as follows.

> ➤ Alert Dialogue Box

> ➤ Confirmation Dialogue Box.

> ➤ Prompt Dialogue Box

Alert Dialog Box

When we want to display a warning message to the users in a dialogue box, then we use an alert dialogue box. E.g., when we validate a form using onsubmit event there we do not accept any input from the user and just need to display a warning message, in this case we use an alert box to display such a warning message. Alert box just has only one "OK" button to click and proceed.

```
<!DOCTYPE html>
<html>
<head>
<meta charset="ISO-8859-1">
<title>On Submit Events</title>
```

```
<script type="text/javascript">
    function validation() {
      if(document.form1.textbox1.value != ''){
            alert('Validation Passed');
            return false;
      }
      else{
            alert ('Text Box field cannot be empty!');
            return false;
      }
    }
</script>
</head>
<body>
    <form name="form1" method="GET" action="onClickEvent.html"
onsubmit="return validation()">
      <input type="text" name="textbox1"/>
      <input type="submit" value="Submit" />
    </form>
</body>
</html>
```

Output

When we execute the above HTML program, the following will be the output. Here, we see an alert dialogue box.

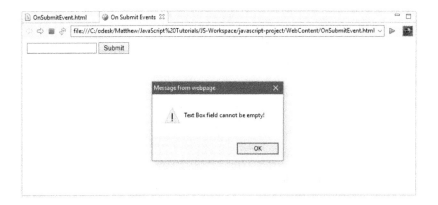

Confirmation Dialog Box

In JavaScript language, a confirmation dialog box is used when we need to take user's opinion on any option. It displays a dialog box that has two buttons: OK button and Cancel button.

When the user clicks on the OK button, then the window method "confirm ()" will return a true value. Otherwise, if the user clicks on the Cancel button, then "confirm ()" method will returns a false value. The following is an example on the confirmation dialogue box.

```
<!DOCTYPE html>
<html>
<head>
<meta charset="ISO-8859-1">
<title>Confirm Box</title>
```

```
<script type="text/javascript">
    function showAlert(){
        confirm ("This is an confirm dialogue box example!");
    }
</script>
</head>
<body>
    <p>Confirm box demo example.</p>
    <input type="button" onclick="showAlert();" value="Call
JavaScript"/>
</body>
</html>
```

Output

When we execute the above HTML program, the following will be the output. Here, we see a confirmation dialogue box.

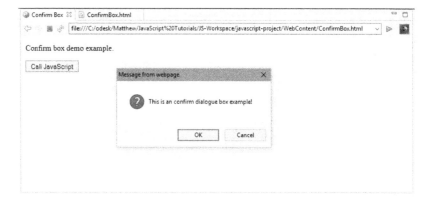

Prompt Dialog Box

In JavaScript language, a prompt dialog box is used when we want to pop-up a text box that accepts the user input. Thus, it allows the system to interact with the user. The user is required to enter the required data into the field and then click on the OK button.

Such a dialog box is displayed by using a method known as *"prompt ()"*. It accepts the following two parameters.

> ➢ A label that we want to display in the text box.

> ➢ A default string which is display in the text box.

The prompt dialog box has the following two buttons.

> ➢ The OK button.

> ➢ The Cancel button.

When the user clicks on the OK button, then the window method *"prompt ()"* will return the value which was entered by the user in the text box. Otherwise, if the user clicks on the Cancel button, then the window method *"prompt ()"* will return a null value.

The following is an example on the prompt dialogue box.

```
<!DOCTYPE html>
<html>
<head>
<meta charset="ISO-8859-1">
```

```
<title>Prompt Box</title>
    <script type="text/javascript">
        function showAlert(){
            prompt ("This is an prompt dialogue box example!");
        }
    </script>
</head>
<body>
    <p>Prompt dialogue box demo example.</p>
    <input type="button" onclick="showAlert();" value="Call
JavaScript"/>
</body>
</html>
```

Output

When we execute the above HTML program, the following will be the output. Here, we see a prompt dialogue box.

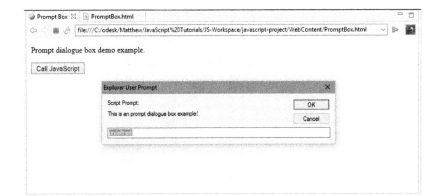

Chapter 14

JavaScript Void Keyword

In JavaScript language, the void keyword can be used as a unary operator which is appeared before its single operand, and may be of any type. This unary operator specifies an expression which is required to be evaluated without any return value.

The following is the syntax and an example of the void keyword.

```html
<!DOCTYPE html>
<html>
<head>
<meta charset="ISO-8859-1">
<title>Void Keyword Example 1</title>
</head>
<body>
    <p>Click here to invoke an alert!</p>
    <a href="javascript:void(alert('Here is the Void Keyword demo'))">Click Here!</a>
</body>
</html>
```

Output

When we execute the above HTML program, the following will be the output. Here, we see an alert dialogue box that popped out on the click of the responsive hyperlink (*"Click Here!"*). On the other hand, if void argument is empty then we see no response as in the case of the second hyperlink (*"No response link!"*) as the expression "0" has no effect in JavaScript. When "0" is evaluated, it does not loads back into the current document.

Alternatively, the void keyword in JavaScript is also used to generate the undefined value as shown in the following example.

```
<!DOCTYPE html>
<html>
<head>
<meta charset="ISO-8859-1">
<title>Void Example 2</title>
    <script type="text/javascript">
```

```
function getVoidDemo(){
    var x,y,z;
    x = void ( y = 50, z = 700 );
    document.write('x = ' + x + ' y = ' + y +' z = ' + z );
}
</script>
</head>
<body>
    <p>Click to get the Result...</p>
    <form>
        <input type="button" value="Get Result" onclick="getVoidDemo();" />
    </form>
</body>
</html>
```

Output

When we execute the above HTML program, the following will be the output. Here the value of the 'x' variable is undefined, however variables 'y' and 'z' has the value as '50' and '700' respectively.

x = undefined y = 50 z = 700

Chapter 15

JavaScript Objects

JavaScript language is an Object Oriented Programming (OOP) based language which provides the following capabilities of OOPs language to the programmer.

> **Encapsulation** – is the concept with which we can store all the related information that includes data and methods, together in an object.

> **Aggregation** – is the concept which enables to store one object inside another object.

> **Inheritance** – is the concept that enables a class to inherit or re-use the properties and the methods of another class (or number of classes). It is also known as parent class.

> **Polymorphism** – is the concept that enables the programmer to write one function/method that execute different task in different ways but defined with the same name. Also known as method overloading.

> **Objects** — are composed of attributes. An attribute can be a function or a property. Function is considered to be a method of the object.

Object Properties in JavaScript

Object properties in JavaScript can be of any of the three primitive data types (Number, String and Boolean), or any of the abstract data types (such as an object). Object properties are the variables which are used internally in the object's methods. They can also be used as globally visible variables therefore, can be used throughout the page. The following is the syntax and the example.

```
<!DOCTYPE html>
<html>
<head>
<meta charset="ISO-8859-1">
<title>Objects Example</title>
    <script type="text/javascript">
        objectName.objectProperty = propertyValue;
        var str = document.title;
    </script>
</head>
<body>

</body>
</html>
```

Here we are assigning the *'propertyValue'* variable value to the object property attribute *'objectProperty'*. The object is referred with the name as *'objectName'*.

In the next statement of the above example, we are storing the value of the *document title* using the *"title"* property of the document object into *"str"* variable.

Object Methods in JavaScript

Objects Methods are the functions with which the object do manipulation or required executions. In JavaScript, the function differs from the method in the following way: A function is a standalone unit of statements whereas a method is attached to an object that can be referenced by the *"this"* keyword.

Methods can be used to display the object contents on the HTML page. They can perform a complex mathematical operations on objects properties attributes and the input parameters passed to the object method. E.g., during this tutorial, we have used the *"write ()"* method of the document object where we pass the string or text as a parameter to be written on the HTML page.

```
<!DOCTYPE html>
<html>
<head>
<meta charset="ISO-8859-1">
<title>Object Method Example</title>
    <script type="text/javascript">
        document.write("Welcome to JavaScript Programming!");
```

```
          </script>
    </head>
    <body>

    </body>
    </html>
```

User-Defined Objects in JavaScript

In JavaScript language, all the user-defined objects as well as the built-in objects extends to an object know as Object (similar to the JAVA language).

The *new* Operator in JavaScript

The *"new"* operator is used for the creation of an object instance. In order to create an object in JavaScript, the statement has the *new* operator which is followed by the constructor method as shown below. Here, the constructor methods are *"Object ()"*, *"Array ()"*, and *"Date ()"*. These constructors are the built-in JavaScript functions.

```
<!DOCTYPE html>
<html>
<head>
<meta charset="ISO-8859-1">
<title>The New Operator</title>
<script type="text/javascript">
        var student = new Object();
```

```
        var languages = new Array("JavaScript", "Pascal", "Python");
        var day = new Date("August 24, 1989");
        alert (day);
</script>
</head>
<body>


</body>
</html>
```

Output

When we execute the above HTML program, the following will be the output. Here, we are displaying the properties of the Date object on the alert dialogue box.

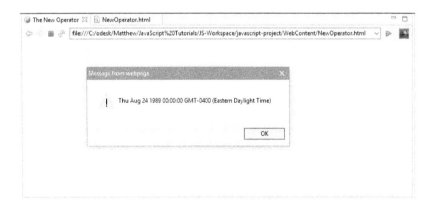

The "Object ()" Constructor

As discussed before, the constructor is a function which creates and initializes a JavaScript object. A special constructor function known as "*Object ()*" is used to build the object in JavaScript. The value returned by the "*Object ()*" constructor is assigned back to a variable known as object reference variable. The following example demonstrates the creation of an Object in JavaScript.

```
<!DOCTYPE html>
<html>
<head>
<meta charset="ISO-8859-1">
<title>Object Creation</title>
<script type="text/javascript">
        var student = new Object();
        student.name = "Appy";
        student.age = "21";
        student.course = "JavaScript";

        function showDetails(){
                alert ("Name: "+student.name+ " Age: "+student.age+" Course:
"+student.course);
        }
</script>
</head>
<body>
        <input type="button" onclick="showDetails();" value="Get Student
```

details!" />

</body>

</html>

This is to be noted that the object properties variables are not defined with the var keyword.

Output

When we execute the above HTML program, the following will be the output.

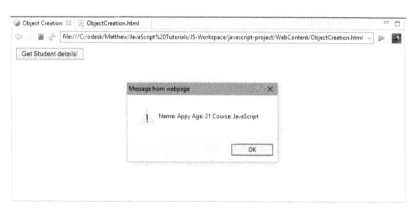

Defining Methods for an Object in JavaScript

In the last example, we have demonstrated to how to use the constructor that creates the object and assigns properties. In the following example, we are going to demonstrate an example to define methods for an object in JavaScript.

```html
<!DOCTYPE html>
<html>
<head>
<meta charset="ISO-8859-1">
<title>Object Methods</title>
<script type="text/javascript">
        function student(name, course){
            this.name = name;
            this.course  = course;
        }
    </script>
</head>
<body>
        <script type="text/javascript">
        var record = new student("Appy", "JavaScript");
        alert("name is : " + record.name + "Course is "+ record.course );
        </script>
</body>
</html>
```

Output

When we execute the above HTML program, the following will be the output. Here, we have added a function along with an object.

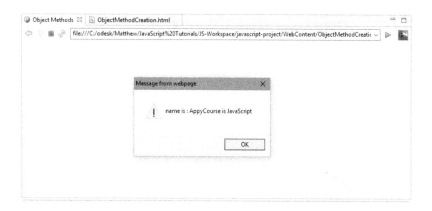

The 'with' Keyword in JavaScript

In JavaScript, the 'with' keyword is used as a shorthand to refer an object's properties or methods.

Here, the object which is specified as an argument to with becomes the default object for the duration of the block that follows. In this case, the properties and methods for the object can be used without naming the object. The following is the syntax and the example.

```
<!DOCTYPE html>
<html>
<head>
<meta charset="ISO-8859-1">
<title>With Keyword</title>
<script type="text/javascript">
    // A function that will work as a method
    function addAge(years){
```

```
        with(this){
           age = years;
        }
     }
     function student(name, course){
        this.name = name;
        this.course  = course;
        this.age = 0;
        this.addAge = addAge; // Property that is a method.
     }
   </script>
</head>
<body>
     <script type="text/javascript">
     var record = new student("Appy", "JavaScript");
     record.addAge(21);
     alert("Name is : " + record.name +
             "\nCourse is : " + record.course +
             "\nAge is : " + record.age );
   </script>
</body>
</html>
```

Output

When we execute the above HTML program, the following will be the output. Here, we have used the *'with'* keyword to add the age later by assigning a method as a property.

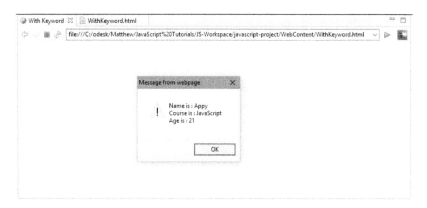

Native Objects in JavaScript

JavaScript language has many built-in or native objects. These native objects can be accessed in the program from anywhere and they will work in the same way on any type of browser that is operating on any type of the operating system. The following are the important JavaScript Native Objects.

➢ JavaScript Array Object.

➢ JavaScript Boolean Object.

➢ JavaScript Date Object.

- ➤ JavaScript Math Object.

- ➤ JavaScript Number Object.

- ➤ JavaScript RegExp Object.

- ➤ JavaScript String Object.

Conclusion

Thank you again for downloading this book!

I hope this book was able to help you learn JavaScript

The next step is to put these practices to work for you.

Thank you and good luck!

Chapter 1

Introduction to Python Programming Language

Did you know websites like YouTube and Dropbox use Python in their source code? Python is a vast language which is easy to understand and apply. You can develop almost anything using Python. Most of the operating systems (Mac, Linux, UNIX, etc.) other than windows have python installed by default. It is an open source and free language. In this eBook, we are going to learn this awesome code language and apply it on various examples. There are no type declaration of methods, parameters, functions or variables (like in other languages) in Python which makes its code short and simple. As mentioned earlier, this language can be used in everything, whether you want to build a website, a game or a search engine. The main advantage of using Python is that you do not have to run compiler explicitly, it is purely interpreted language like Perl or Shell.

File extension which is used by Python source file is ".py" and it is a case-sensitive language, so "P" and "p" would be considered as two different variables. Also, Python figures out the variable type on its own, for example, if you put x=4 and y='Python' then it will consider x as integer and y as string. We are going to learn all these basics in detail in further chapters. Before moving forward, few important points to remember are:

1. For assigning a value "=" is used and for comparison "==" is used. Example, x=4, y=8, x==y

2. "print" is used to print results.

3. All the mathematical operations like +, -, *, /, % are used with numbers

4. Variable is created when a value is assigned to it. Example, a=5 will create a variable named "a" which has an integer value of 5. There is no need to define it beforehand.

5. "+" can also be used to concatenate two string. Example, z= "Hi", z= z + "Python"

6.For logical operations "and", "or", "not" are used instead of symbols.

There are three basic data types: integer (by default for numbers), floats (a=3.125) and string. String can be defined either by "" (double quotes) or single quotes (''). We are going to see all the datatypes with proper examples in upcoming chapters.

Let's look at the step by step guide to install Python on Windows operating system. As mentioned earlier, if you are using other operating system like UNIX or Linux or Mac then Python should be installed already and ready to use. You have to use "%python" to get the details on Linux, press "CTRL + D" to exit. For running it on UNIX, "%python filename.py" is used. Python prompts with three "greater than" symbol (>>>).

Click here to check out the rest of Python Programming on Amazon.

Or go to: http://amzn.to/2auRjNy

www.ingramcontent.com/pod-product-compliance
Lightning Source LLC
Chambersburg PA
CBHW071221050326
40689CB00011B/2396